Don't Tell Me Not to Ask Why

Also by Samantha King Holmes

Born to Love, Cursed to Feel
We Hope This Reaches You in Time (with r.h. Sin)

Don't Tell Me Not to Ask Why

Poetry & Prose

Samantha King Holmes

Andrews McMeel
PUBLISHING®

To my husband, thank you for always seeing me

Let the Children Speak

Let's not talk about it
Let's not address it
The lump under the rug still has more room

As a child, I was taught not to speak
I was young, what did I know
As an adult, I was still told not to speak out,
it's disrespectful
Didn't I turn out fine despite the circumstances,
wasn't that enough?
You said your best was given
That's a lie I'm no longer able to accept
I was the one who had to live with the
consequences of adult decisions
that didn't have my best interest in mind
You should have just listened
You defend yourself, you justify,
where you should apologize

You treat me as if there is still milk on my breath
while expecting an adult to grow from the ashes
of my adolescence
Expecting no tears to be shed over the desolation
of my childhood

I think we've created a reality
where we just don't talk about what came before
We avoid the potholes of our bonds
We stopped trying to fill them in long ago
So little hope for recovery

Is it a shock I've kept my mouth shut so long?
Endured, suffered quietly
As if my pain, my anguish had no place
in this world
Didn't deserve to be spoken, acknowledged
What power I gave everyone over me
with my devoted silence
I think my childhood died there
That's what dire circumstances do to you
You're a child seeing life through a child's eyes,
being called to be mature enough to handle a
situation, but not have an opinion
How confusing that our maturity should merely be a
convenience when called upon but struck down the
minute it's pointed out the hand they've played in it
They never want to hear the truth
even when we've aged and deserve answers

How hard it must be to face the product of your not so
well thought out decisions in a living, breathing form that
continues to ask questions that you don't feel the need to answer
It's easy to point out my mistakes without taking
into consideration how you contributed in making
me who I am
I'm not looking for perfection here
or even an apology
I've wanted the truth for so long

and now must accept that's not something
you're willing to give me

If Only

Guess we should have talked more
Guess you should have listened
I guess you should have taken the time
to make more of an effort
I guess things would be different
if that were the case
My feelings are valid
My truth is loud
I've somehow learned to drown out
the past with the beat of my ambitions
Guess you made me stronger
Guess I should thank you
Truth is though
you should have just loved me

Wet Blanket

I remember our house was big
So big, in fact, that I trapped myself there
I don't think I ever quite forgave you for all that
we lost or keeping from me what actually went
wrong
Everything happened so fast
I've worked so hard the majority of my life
to have that house, to have that life back,
without ever asking myself if that's what I really
needed
I think all I really wanted was what
I was made to believe is fulfilling
I tried to keep us all intact
Stay, be the family we're supposed to be
I guess life is filled with humor
even when I don't want to see it
Everyone just wanted their own lives
I think we're all just figuring it out
So that house with the honeysuckle that grows in
the back is something I have to let go of
I didn't get to keep it then
and I don't need it now
It wasn't filled with anything that lasted
I have to create my own space

Just Call Me Alice

I always escaped into books,
out of windows, and into my daydreams
I left behind a reality I felt
I was too young to change
They mocked me and my moods,
chalked it up to the transition
No one acknowledged the pain, the scars,
the desire to be home even though I didn't
rightfully have one to call my own
I became something different
I stowed away into the nooks of a library,
the corner of any room
I wasn't hiding myself from the world,
just working out my place in it
Carving out a reality that I felt
I would one day belong in
They may have thought it was silly of me to
dream, but my reality now is better than anything
I created in my mind

Never Enough

I could never tell you
how when you called me stocky
it made me insecure
I could never tell you
I stopped eating to be smaller
I could never tell you
I started to embrace my body
after boys noticed me
I could never tell you
they broke my heart too
I could never tell you
that I envied daughters
who had a relationship with their mother
I could never tell you
I wanted that too
I could never tell you
I felt like you chose him over us
I could never tell you
how much it all hurt
The destruction I allowed my body,
soul, and mind to go through
I could never tell you
what I've endured as a woman
There's so much you don't know
And even though you're in my life now
there's still so many things I still can't tell you

Cruel Intentions

The first people to make me love
my body were boys

Even after I had cut them off
they left their intentions on me
pumping through my veins like venom
I became addicted to the validation
taking chances with my heart
I shouldn't have chased them

I think men enjoyed the thought
of taming something wild
My body became the final frontier
They decimated me,
and left it up to me to rebuild
I don't think I ever blossomed the same
There are scars that fleck the
beauty of what's left
I feel like they used me as an escape
A momentary lapse of lust confused as
genuine affection

Lynbrook Motel

I remember the way it smelled
It was dry, decaying,
reeked of hopelessness and neglect
It stuck to your nostrils, clung to your clothes
as if you were its only chance for salvation
The decor was out of date
It's the stuff made of movies
We shouldn't be here
How strange, home went from walls in a house
to a room we occupy for $100 a day
Don't call us resilient, I think we were just numb
Just getting by
Just getting through it
That wasn't home
Just a space in time that spurred everything else

———————

I don't think you ever really liked me
We were obligated by blood to protect
to lean on, to be there for,
but liking someone is a choice
I've been brave, I've been strong, but I don't
know if you ever respected me
I came along, and it was another person
to steal the attention away
Another person to be matched up against
I think you've always looked for in others
what I was supposed to be
I think you found a good replacement
I don't know what made you hate me so much
or why you feel the need to compete
I've been far from perfect
but my decisions are my own
It's hard for people to accept
that our relationship has changed
become nonexistent
but I think it is time to accept
that just because we're family
doesn't mean we'll be friends

224th

I remember the smell of honeysuckle
and the tickle of overgrown grass
My fingers outstretched toward the sun
the heat of it lingering on the tips
This little girl with so much in front of her
I go back to her, to that moment
The innocence, the dreamer,
before reality creeped in to show her
how strong she truly was, had to be
She didn't know pain yet
She knew nothing of a relentless
need or want of others
She was happy there all alone in the tall grass
left with her imagination and the warmth on her
skin

Hindsight

You both checked out
Our childhood became collateral damage
That's a depressing way to think about it
I don't think anyone ever asked if I was angry
I'm still angry
There was no time to debrief
We had to keep going, always going
No time for questions, no time to understand
If I stopped for too long
it would bear down on me like a storm
Everything I'd been avoiding
So, we just kept running
I fought my storms alone
Retreated inside of people, delusions
As if somehow, if I loved someone enough
and it was returned, then everything
would be fine

I got that wrong
Love of self had to come first
The right person followed after

Liliane

I wish one day to be half the woman you were
I look more like you the older I get, so I hope I'm
off to a good start
I remember the last conversation we had
I vaguely remember your smile and your laugh
Your ascension occurred when I was young
My mind refuses to recall the images of your
body giving way on you
Your soul gently saying goodbye to the frame that
encased it
I catch a familiar scent of you and it makes me
want to cry
I never got to tell you how grateful I am that you
were in my life
With age came the understanding of the
unrelenting love you gave
With faith came the acknowledgment that
you're in a better place
I hope when you look down that you are proud
I'm doing my best

Boden Ave

The scent of fresh baked cookies, the thud of
children running, and laughter fill the house
The pizza you ordered is on its way
The living room floor a mosaic of comforters
for the sleepover
There are debates over what scary movie to play
The atmosphere is dripping in a warmth and love
that comes from all of us being together once again
I've come to see this place as an uplifting refuge
A refreshing break from the constant worry on
my mind and the things I'm not saying
I get to be myself, I get to be honest, and the
amount of affection that gets poured over us in
this home is overwhelming
There is no such thing as overstaying our
welcome
You treat us as if we're your own children even
though we're not
You've always stood tall, always have made us
feel safe
I may not have said this enough
but thank you for being a constant light in our
lives and for always going that extra mile
I know you didn't have to

I'm just not there yet

I'm learning I don't need
your truth to move forward
It won't fix anything
I caged myself in a past that
I wanted you to change
I fooled myself into believing that
you owning up would
somehow make things right
The truth is, I just haven't forgiven you
I haven't been able to accept who you are
and the choices you've made
I don't know how

It's time to face it

We stick to the surface
Venturing too deep means the possibility
of disturbing old wounds and facing issues
we're still not comfortable talking about
The cure of which would be time and distance
until talking on the phone no longer seemed
like an obligation

I think we've gone the avoidance
route for far too long
We no longer know how to connect
Now that we don't speak anymore
I've become ok with that
At first it hurt, but I've become solidified in the
notion that someone doesn't just get to treat me
poorly and get away with it
We should have been honest or just gotten help
I think we're at a place
where repairing takes too much out of us
We no longer see this as a bond worth saving

Trophy Child

I hate that you tell people about me
That you put me in situations
where I meet them
They approach and tell me how
they feel like they know me
How can they?
You barely do
At least not the way you should
Most times I don't even know who they are
I end up feeling like a prop in a scene
that I'm just waiting to be over
You're selling what they willingly buy into
No need to question why I'm a bit standoffish
Have you told them that before this we hadn't
talked in weeks?
That we don't spend the holidays together
We haven't really for years
No?
What about the chaos we endured when we were
younger?
Did any of what made me who I am ever get
explained?
I hate the lies, all the lies,
especially the one where we pretend
like we're all one big happy, healthy family
I spare your feelings constantly
even though it's not my job
So, I stand still and stare off
as you gush over everything I've become
without explaining the part you played in it

We are accomplices in letting people believe
that you did something to encourage me
Truth is though . . .
Well I guess, who really cares what the truth is

Acceptance

I think I yearned for something that
hadn't quite held me in its embrace
Who taught my soul there was something
more to yearn for?
I always knew something was missing but could
never teach someone the right way to fill
in the empty space

Acceptance has been my shortcoming
for longer than I've been aware
I didn't see, wouldn't acknowledge, your pain
I only cared about mine and the role you were
supposed to play in my life
I get that there's more to what happened
than I can recall
It's just a shame the love you felt you were
missing is exactly what you starved me of
Exiling me to roam through every door that
opened without a thought of what was waiting for
me on the other side
You didn't see me; I didn't see you

I guess you felt abandoned
Can you see the irony?
In the life you chose to lead and how
that ultimately affected me
In the way you've remained silent
As if speaking about things
would rock the boat and toss us over
You hate confrontation

I rush to protect, it normally doesn't
work out to my best interest
I always felt the need to defend myself
because you didn't do it enough
I wish you did, you were supposed to be my
shield from the world and all the bad people in it

I know I have to forgive your broken pieces
It's just, you were supposed to be the benchmark
that I measure myself up to
The best I can do is admit that I'm not quite
at that point yet
I'm starting to accept that you have your own
stories, truths too excruciating to speak aloud
You just don't have the heart
I needed you all and felt like I was failed
I get it, you weren't made to be perfect
I'll move forward, I'll get past this
I'm trying, just know I'm trying

Ancestry

I'm digging at the roots, bare hands
fingers bleeding, torn skin, raw flesh
Tell me her name
Tell me everything you're hiding
that you think I can't handle
I barely know the branches, give me the roots
Was there someone like me?
How did her life turn out?
Why is a lack of information always seen as safe?
How many skeletons are buried out here?
Do you really want me to find out on my own?

Branches, I think I hate these branches
They're full of lies and secrets
I think the foundation is dying
finally poisoned by all the hate
All the horrible things left unspoken
Everything is just falling away
I want the truth
I need something deeper, I have to unearth it
Dig it all up on my own
That means being the one to
expose what no one else is willing to
How lucky for me to be brave

Unearthed

She said my name
and it was like it was being reintroduced to me
That first conversation she told me she loved me
even though she doesn't know me
I don't doubt it
It was probably one of the most genuine times
it's been said to me in my life by a stranger
We didn't talk long, but enough for me
to know that there's more to the story
Despite what may come
I did the right thing by calling her
and letting her know I exist

I shouldn't have called

I knew that it was over
the moment after I hung up
The spillover was too great
That's the thing about bottling it up
your issues don't wait for you to be ready
They rattle your bones, ignite your blood
Mine came out in pleading heaves and sobs,
a confession unheard
The truth and the pain mixed in a dance,
twirling around the inevitable
It happened so fast
If words can create worlds
then we built a universe
only to destroy it with our anger
Things won't ever be the same
I don't know when the lies stop
Maybe when you become more solidified
in who you are or maybe
when they stop being easy to swallow
I was no longer this little girl who
needed to be picked up or saved
Just to be listened to, heard, respected
Respect, it's such an interesting word
I don't think any of you would ever be
able to see me that way
As someone who deserved yours
As something more than the tiny person
who doesn't know what she's doing with her life
What I need now is something you can't supply
you haven't ever really

That is something both of us will just
have to live with

Next in Line

I don't know what I did to make you hate me
but you have for such a long time
Maybe you feel like you got swindled by life
Skipped over by its favor
You were the center of attention
for such a short time
Eventually I came along
and every eye cast itself upon me
I was braver, bolder, clever,
some would say a bit reckless
People would tell me
what I couldn't do or have
and yet somehow
I would bend things to my will
Here I am talking about myself
and therein lies the problem I guess
Others did the same
You got lost in the mayhem
became the responsible leader
Pretty much did everything first
No one could tell you anything
Your way was the right way
even when it wasn't
But somehow, I became the one to transcend
all doubts, assumptions, ill will thrown my way
I'm the next head of this matriarchy
I gather, I coordinate, I keep things together
I take on the responsibility
I'm the one with power
I see how this could upset you

How you may even feel robbed
I'm not going to apologize for who I'm becoming
I'm going to be strong and I will lead well
I didn't have to be here alone
You thought it would be better to be against me
rather than stand side by side
You should have paid attention
I'm the one you should have bet on

Lighten the Load

It's like I want to rip the negative emotions
out and imprison them on a page
I just want them to stop living inside me

My Secret Sadness

I sink into this abyss and say nothing
Cradled in between I don't feel
anything and everything
I guess that's denial
I want to cry
I'm dying on the inside for something
I'm just not quite sure what
It's like waking from a nightmare
unable to recall the details but still scared
That's where I am
That's where I've been
I've been trying to tell myself
I'm not sad for so long that for a time I fooled
myself into believing that I'm all right
I don't know how to tell you
I don't even think I want to

Tangled in Your Web

There are some days where you act
like I'm the love of your life
others it seems like you hate me
I've stopped asking myself which
outweighs the other

Renewal Denied

Everything became tainted
I think we've argued in every room
There isn't a corner I can tuck myself
into and seek refuge
I don't think you decided to up
and hate me overnight
It took time
I've become silent, drowned out
This place just doesn't have enough space
The silence is thick, always so thick
It's suffocating
The sound of my sobs an aggressive intrusion
I don't know how we got here
I don't know how we'll get out
We can't stay here
We don't belong here

Prey

I wonder what they saw when they looked at me
Could they tell I was in dire need of feeling loved?
Is desperation a scent they got off of me?
Did they know they could rip me apart and I
wouldn't fight?
That only the bare minimum needed to be
given for me to stay
Lies and deception wouldn't be a deterrent
That despite their faults, I would give my all
Make them feel like they were a
priority in my life
I wonder if who I was and what I would allow to
happen was something they always knew

I can't bear your judgment

No one knows how bad this hurts
and I won't tell them
'cause I know I'm going to stay
and I don't feel like being judged for it

———————

Abandoned, feels like my life is in disarray
I patiently wait for the storm to stop
It relentlessly pours in waves
The sun peeks, but never comes out
How many times do I need to mess
up a good thing?
I sit at the window and stare, envisioning
happiness dancing along the grass
Playfully combing through my hair
like a strong wind
This anguish is all knowing, all encompassing
Whose wrath have I evoked?
What punishment is mine to bear?
This experience that I am meant to gain, must it
really be so painful?
Am I that strong-willed that I must be broken to
become more resilient?
So many questions lie within the eye of turmoil
Silence, I only crave the sweet serenity
of a silent mind
I can no longer take the constant playbacks
of all that has been lost
The ruins of my past haunt me
A history I know by heart, but haven't learned
from properly
Breathe
I inhale and exhale, but find so little relief
It's me, I know it now
It's me
My joy gets swept under the current

of my desire for perfection
I hold on to what I know is bad for me
Haunted by my reflection, I see who I was
and not who I am
It's me, the storm is me and it will never stop
Not until my desire to be happy alone supersedes
my need to be loved by others

Bottled Up

Sometimes there are no words
for the emotions you feel
No way to describe it or get it out
So, you just sit there while a storm
wreaks havoc inside of you
No one notices, 'cause if they could
see it, they would pay attention

The kindest thing you did was leave

I fear asking for more
because I know you won't give it
What is knowledge to a mind that isn't open?
What is wisdom to ears that won't listen?
Waiting for a phone call that doesn't come
Believing in feelings that were never professed
Hoping for sentiments that don't exist
I have to admit that I'm at my worst when I'm
with you

I only ever wanted to be the person you loved
Not simply the one you lay beside
I deserve that, better
I've treated you as if you were
confined in my life, trapped in my veins
Making your way in and out of my heart

I've split myself open to please you to no avail
I knew you wanted to leave
I was just trying to keep you from going
You served your purpose
I just couldn't stand to accept that
there was nothing left for us
You were a dream I didn't want to end
So, you ended it for me

_____

He doesn't love me anymore
I think he prefers the vision of me
he created in his mind
Reality set in
I don't fit the mold
My flaws are too real
My shortcomings too great
It happened over time, the disdain
At first it was small, but then it grew roots
Every new discovery only adding
a bloom to our downfall

They always say transitions are hard
They just forget to mention how
it washes over your entire being
I can't pretend like this isn't all different

I don't think you ever really missed me
I don't think you ever really cared
It probably just sounded good rolling off your
tongue and making its way to your ears
I don't think you ever really thought of me
Somehow it was my responsibility to keep
something going that you didn't
care enough to nurture
I'm at a loss over how easy it was
for you to detach
I shouldn't be
You gave me no illusions
You just happened to benefit
from the ones I created

The Relationship Misconception

You get told you're nothing long enough
the objective becomes to prove that
you're worthy
Hurt me, I'll stay just to show you
I deserve better treatment
I'm going to be so good to your negligence, your
verbal abuse, your inability to be loyal,
that you're going to have to open your eyes to the
kind, strong, patient woman that I am
I'm going to show you I'm worth something
despite the fact that you've given me nothing

Searching for the Light

They say to find the beauty in your suffering
How?
When you're wrapped in your grief
When you're trying to steal breaths
through the sobs
Where is this beauty?
In the ghosts of tears upon your face
In the way the world seems to slow down
ensuring you feel every dreadful minute of it
Staring off for hours, riddled with an
overwhelming sea of emotions,
unable to release them
Still haven't found it

———————

"You're weak" pounded
on either side of my head
Searing my mind, seeping down into my bones
I felt the weight of it
I had been weak for men
who never really loved me
Weak for friends who didn't appreciate me
Even weak for family who wouldn't
acknowledge the pain they caused
With you, though, I didn't think
of myself that way
I always thought I was something more
Now you see me as they do
As they always have
Who knew all it would take is
two words to rip apart my reality

I don't know if things will get better
We've crossed a threshold unexplored
before into uncharted emotions
It seems we've reached our limit
Both damaged, both angry, both in need
of time and space from the other
I don't fear us not making our way back
We've both moved forward with living
I think that's something we do best separately
No fear of judgment
No brace for criticism
No need to keep things to ourselves
There is no illusion here that
we bring each other happiness
I think my resolve scares you
Your view of me is disconcerting
I don't know where this is all landing
We've taken too much from each other
Too much pain, too much animosity
not enough forgiveness

Don't tell me to smile

Stop telling me to smile
Stop devouring me with your eyes
Stop following me down the street,
yelling after me, as if you're entitled to my time
Stop trying to force me to believe that I need to
stop and entertain your desires
I'm not obligated to give you what you want
Respect my right to exist without your attention
Respect my right to feel safe
to explore my city, this world, without feeling like
with each glance I'm in danger
Stop telling me I stole your heart
Stop trying to taint my moments of peace
Stop making it seem like I have to be nice to you
all because you want to have a conversation
I've been catcalled, pursued by men
since the tender age of eleven
That shouldn't have happened
My body being blamed for
their lack of self-control
It wasn't my fault
I remember wearing baggy clothes to hide my
figure in the hopes that no one would notice me
I allowed others to make me want
to feel invisible
I'm tired
It's been well over a decade, almost two
For years I've dealt with it, still deal with this
Stop making it seem like it's me, like it's us
Stop forcing me to hold you accountable

To My Vessel

I've ached for you to be different
Wished that you would change
to the picture I have in my mind
I've languished at your curvaceousness,
cringed at your sway
As if it was your fault for the invasion
men's eyes made, make
It wasn't, still isn't
I've wanted you to be smaller here, bigger there,
tucked in here, more polished
I've abused you far worse than
any lustful bystander
I'm sorry
You have always been strong even if that isn't the
aspect that was acknowledged
You deserved, deserve, better from me
To be loved, appreciated
Thank you for standing tall
when I wanted to crumble
For everything we've come through together
You are beautiful
It's about time I told you that

Boiling Point

There was an ache in my chest
Anger rumbling in my belly
I've shut my mouth for so long it
finally caught up with me
I remember the day I erupted
It all came rushing out
Uncontrollable, uncensored, a storm of rage
demolishing everything in its path
My emotions clawed at the back
of my throat, climbing
in desperate need for my voice to give them life
It was too much
Months of pretending came to a halt
I think my range of emotions
makes other people uncomfortable, so I lie
I act like I'm ok, as if everything is fine
so they can go on in their happy delusion
I give them what they want at my expense
They don't care; it's not their sacrifice
I've reduced myself to this, a people pleaser
It must have been shocking
when I said I didn't want to anymore
I know it made you sad
It didn't bring me pleasure
I can no longer compromise
just to make others happy, don't ask me to

Delusion

I wasn't happy
I was just pretending
I was drowning myself in the liquor, the music,
the dancing, the strangers
It was empty, all of it
I was lost, I think they knew it
I tried to make myself fit where I didn't belong
all 'cause I wanted to feel alive
None of those things and
none of those people did it for me
It was a lie I allowed myself to be told,
forced myself to believe
The truth at that time was a scary thing to face
I wasn't happy and nothing I did was fixing that
It was me, the unhappiness was inside me
and I didn't know how to change that
I made it look like I was living
when the truth is I always felt so alone

A Poison Called Silence

I think I push things down
Drive them down so deep that they
get buried and then grow inside me
Wrapping themselves around my bones
killing me from the inside

Social

I'm obsessed with my phone
and all the people who live in it
I have never been so connected to others
and so disconnected from myself

Writer's Block

I became so concerned with perception
that I lost a piece of myself that
I'm still trying to find
It took my words with it
I'm left barren
My emotions drowning in their own
selfish need to be heard
Do you really need me?
I know I need you
I've scoured my mind to see if you're hiding
Tucked away in some crevice of my subconscious
that I've chosen to ignore
I've tried to call upon you
You used to come so easily
Now there is nothing
Just emptiness and this yearning
to have you in my life again

I don't think you truly know what it costs
to be this honest, this vulnerable
You think you want it, say you want it
knowing nothing of the sacrifice
The torture you put yourself through
by constantly reliving a moment
till you can get it out right
Get it out the way you need it to be heard
The toll it takes on you
There is no quick fix, no simple remedy
You just move on to the next moment that
overwhelms you enough to capture it

Deception

I sigh into the reality that things won't change
People have run out of ideas
so they raid my mind
trample on my soul
revel in my secrets
then speak them into the world
as if they are their own
As if their back was broken under the hands of a
man tormented by his demons
As if their body was used
and discarded when convenient
I see it now like I saw it then, the lies
in black and white for all the world
to see and admire
They hold no satisfaction for me,
not even temporary
I've given my body, I've given my soul
I just didn't know my story would be taken,
diminished, and fall off the lips of those who are
not worthy of the pain I've endured to share it

Who will save the healers?

I get it now
Why the creatives get overwhelmed,
stuck in that dark place
They give, and give, and give
but keep so little for themselves
We are captivated by their words
Intrigued by their pain,
but we don't heal them
We can't

Dreams Aren't Free

What's your price?
What would you give to hand over your life?
Give me your essence, let me clone you
Hand me the shards of your broken,
let me own you then sell you to the world
Give me your scars, your virtue
ripped to shreds, your innocence betrayed
Everything that's made you a sensation, a phenomenon, a force
to admire
Give me your price so I can sell you a dream and show you have
no value

I Shouldn't Have Let You In

There were never enough gifts
Never enough apologies to bandage
the wounds, so they kept leaking
I began to give way to a version of me
that needed your approval
You loved me broken
That didn't make sense then, still doesn't
With each fight, I was sculpted, shaped
A piece of me ticked away until all that remained was who you
always wanted
You didn't love her either

I always give too much, too soon

I don't think anyone can help me this time
I've been overtaken by the rage
coursing through my veins like a fire
I'm being ripped apart
My vulnerabilities fully exposed
You weren't important
You aren't important
I made you important
It was all me
I made up my mind that you were, are,
something that you're not
I could say that I hate you
but I hate me more

Night falls, and the wounds we try
to pretend we don't have begin to haunt us

You're stronger than you know
Life is a constant cycle, time never ceasing
Consistently enduring when we believe we can't
I know the pain you feel knows no boundaries
to the point where numbness is your constant
state of living
Gravitate toward all that's good in your life
For you alone are an infinite possibility
Begin a new chapter
Leave behind all your doubts
A trail of pieces of a broken heart and tissues
will not do on this journey
Wide-eyed, open-minded, and fearless
you must begin
Crawling till the thought of standing alone
no longer seems unnerving
For living is something we ought to do
but often forget to

Codependent

Living in her shadow
Your growth is restricted
You don't care
You'd give anything for the moments
around her where you feel alive
Despite how temporary or superficial they are
You don't know who you are without her
It doesn't matter who you were before
You feel powerless to her charm and
let her snide comments roll off your back
telling yourself it's just her humor
She makes you feel like you need her
She's the life of the party
She's the reason people pay attention to you
She's what makes you feel special
What's not being said is that without you
she feels like nothing
She admires your fearlessness, your talent
Your search for your purpose
The way you laugh loudly, enjoy life
If you weren't around, there would be no one to
tell her how beautiful she is and mean it
She needs you more than you need her
She just can't let you see that

Too Much History

Your voice is still ringing in my ears
I think that was the most honest
we've been in a long time
Just harsh words scathing at skin
Seeing who'll rip open first
I think I did
We were straightforward
Shouldn't that feel good?
The weight of it all pressing down on me
You probably didn't even feel it
That's what my good heart got me
More people than not who just
don't give a damn
We were friends
I think we're broken
Neither of us wants to repair it

_____

I'm tired of making myself inferior
just to make you important
I eased up on my pace
scared I would leave you behind
only to then watch you walk past me
You will always put yourself first
I'm paralyzed in this state of mind
unable to do the same
Forsake my bleeding heart
It has only brought me pain

Putting Me First

I feel like my soul is made up of dead leaves,
broken promises, and bottles of denial
I've drowned myself in
I wanted to keep every one
Expense mattered not
I sacrificed myself, over and over
for this dream of perfection
The perfect family, the perfect relationship
I was so concerned about holding
everyone else together
I didn't give myself a chance
Ask what I wanted out of this life
I just let everyone else tell me
I was trying to give myself what
I didn't grow up with, stability
No one told me to stop
I should've stopped
I explored the wrong spaces
with the wrong people
I let them disgrace my good intentions
with their need to feel powerful by crushing me
I was merely entertainment
Their hands didn't deserve to make
my body their sanctuary
They left me to find myself in the rubble

Let's just throw salt on my wounds
Let's pretend like it was Love
Betrayal has been too real lately
The pain is so fresh
The healing process hasn't started yet
Who was I to believe that it had?
I give and give and give till there
is no peace left for me
I nod my head, I say yes, and
I let you destroy me
I pick up the pieces after you're gone
Foolish enough to want you to come back
even if it means I'll bleed some more
Let the blood run, I am used to its color
It's when I'm not hurting that I am lost
Isn't it a shame when the only interaction that
you're accustomed to is dysfunction?
You sparked this in me
You'll never even know it
I sit here in a daze
I thought you were different
I really believed it
You were just better disguised
It seems I attract my punishment
It feels so good at first until it doesn't
then I'm left in this rut
Stuck between why it didn't work and wanting to
feel something besides the constant agony
I made you important

Before that you were simply an amusement to be
enjoyed and even sometimes neglected
I gave your presence meaning in my life
You didn't have to work for

_____

I've tied my happiness to
people and items for too long
I've waited for others to let me
feast upon their love
without having any for myself

You didn't say anything
just walked right past me
It was like I didn't even exist
If you had looked back, even for a second
you would see how much you broke me with
your disregard
It was etched on my face
In the constant rise and fall of my chest
as I tried to breathe through completely falling
apart
But you didn't
Does "I love you" mean anything anymore?
Did it ever?

———————

We have to be mindful of not only the love we
say we're giving but also the type we allow
ourselves to receive

Self-Defeat

I always make the mistake of
looking over, looking around
then I look inward and start to pick
apart all the beautiful pieces of myself
I could change this
This could be better
I could try this
As if everything outside of this vessel
I harbor is so much more
That it is I who must change to fit it
I'd really rather not make that mistake anymore

In My Brown Skin

I know when you ask me if I need help
that you don't mean it
I don't know what you're searching my eyes for
There is no mischief that will reveal itself to you
I came here with a purpose in mind
Soon enough I'm being followed
in a way that's less than discreet
It's just like that time
when we were followed around a
bookstore by a security guard
He didn't know that we were just Authors
trying to find our books to sign
It gets tiring
This dance of accusation and defense
You assume who I am and somehow
it's up to me to clarify that I'm different

You'll say it's not about color
That we make everything about color
That you're tired of hearing about it
How convenient that you only get to
be tired of hearing about it

How am I to explain it if discrimination hasn't
gripped you by the shoulders and shaken your
faith in humanity?
It's a heaviness that clings to your back
and rides it all day

It sits on your mind scrambling to rationalize why
it happened to you
There must have been something that could have
been done differently
Anger-filled tears stream down your face as you
know you are not to blame for a prejudice
created before you came into existence

Why is my skin automatically seen as such an
offense?
Painted out as a good enough reason to be
judged
I respect my husband, he experiences it
so much more and somehow remains
patient in the face of it
I smile when I'm with him, so he won't seem
threatening, so I won't seem threatening
As eyes question why we're in this space
Our presence here for some reason
needs justification
Is there no space we're entitled to?
I shouldn't have to smile just to make you
comfortable
Your fear of us is more of a threat to our safety
than we are to you
Haven't you figured that out yet?

The rage of keeping quiet builds inside of me
and I end up taking it out on those who don't
deserve it, but I can't speak up
If I do, you'll just call me angry
an emotion that gets slung around as an insult

Am I only allowed to feel what you want me to?
Speak in a tone that doesn't unnerve you?
There's nothing progressive about trying to
censor how someone is allowed to feel

We always have to be better than the way
others treat us
Always have to be an example when we
want to defend ourselves
I'm still learning how to look past people
and their negative views
Preventing their hate from getting rooted
under my skin

How someone views you doesn't define you
Don't carry the weight of their assumptions, the
labels they place on you
They don't deserve to taint your innocence

I thought about not having this poem
put in the book, but this is my story,
our story
I have every right to tell it
even if you don't want to listen

I remember the moment of my undoing
One string was all it took
and there it was all on the floor
The misery, the resentment, the anger
I finally let it all go
I carried it for so long, too long
It was better without me reliving every single
moment that I couldn't change or accept
The people who wouldn't love me
no matter how hard I loved them
The ones who were hateful because
they knew no other way
The abandonment, the jealousy, the
manipulation
The lack of guidance
You gave me to the world
and let it have its way
I survived it, became braver,
and decided to thrive
I think I've done a good job

———————

I feel so broken
I am going to make something
really great out of that

———————

Be mindful of what you decide to entangle your happiness with. You may find it doesn't provide you with what you need. It's so much deeper than surface level.

The Pursuit of Perfection

No one understands how crippling it is
The devastating fear
The recurrence of negative thoughts
played on a loop, haunting me
I have failed my mind with my impulsive need
to analyze every word, every gesture
I am relentless
It has drained me of the ability
to simply be present in a moment
I don't get to enjoy; I need to control it

I gave up before I even got out
of bed that morning
I had no fight left
I lay there for a while
chained to the thought
that today would be no better

Is Anyone Being Honest?

I don't want to get out of bed
Here, I'm safe
I'm avoiding starting the day
My sheets and cover are magic
as long as I'm wrapped in them
I won't have to face what's waiting for me
The sun's radiance now feels like an invasion
It's calling for me to be happy
and I'm failing to meet the expectation
The mere thought of joy is unbearable
It should be raining, I want the rain
For now, I'll just hide here, block it all out
I don't want to get up
I can't let my feet touch the floor, or the pain
I've been avoiding will surely meet them
I don't think people really care
They say they understand the sadness
without knowing how deep it goes
How many people are truly happy?

_____

What is this urge we have to fix what we feel is broken in someone else and not ourselves?

Human Resources

Passion driven in a direction of revenge
Trying to prove that I was always better
than who they made me out to be
What were once the right intentions
are now tainted
Poisoned by a selfish need to be seen, known,
respected
My age has increased and brought with it
a tidal wave of anxiety and doubt
Who am I becoming?
Watching everyone else's dreams come to
fruition only helped establish that I haven't
a grasp on mine
The commute plus my nine-to-five is draining
I let life's moments idle
I got a whiff of stability and became content
I was meant for something
Isn't that what we're searching for?
I'm ambition deficient trying to find myself
I'm going to be great, extraordinary
You just wait and see
Once I figure out who I'm supposed to be

———————

We wake up every morning
to an existence we squander
So used to the routine
we live for anything that deviates
from the norm, doing more harm than good
We look at what we don't have in envy
I'm a good person, I deserve that
but aren't willing to take the strides
and make the sacrifices to get it
Let's let reality check in for a moment
We'd all rather live in a dream
'cause that makes life slightly easier to bear

Growth Has a Cost

This is such a tough place, so lonely
They told me there would be sacrifices
Who knew for others it would be me
My dreams are no longer a refuge
The monsters meet me there
What is to be done when you are no
longer a person to others?
Just another object to be used
repeatedly till the value runs out
It's such a lonely place when the circle
of who you can trust gets smaller

Rose

You are more than just my friend
You are essential in my life
Your level of kindness is unmatched
You never judge no matter the circumstance
You are always resolute, reassuring
Our bond is almost a decade strong
We've talked about being old ladies
who sit and reminisce and also wreak havoc
If there is anything we share in abundance, its
laughter
Talking for hours about our day
and the luck you have with odd occurrences
There isn't a need to argue for us
There is no conflict
I respect your opinion and you respect mine
We don't always have to agree
The first person to get a phone call or an update
Family isn't just about blood, but knowing
who you can rely on
I know I can depend on you for anything
I don't doubt how much you care
or if I need you that you'll be by my side
Thank you for being the anomaly that you are

Second Hand

You saw value where others
saw used and I saw damaged
The pages turned so easily for you
No chapter left unread
Your face never revealed a bit of judgment
It was constantly tinged with empathy and a bit
of anger at the unsavory treatment
You saw character, knowledge, and strength
Held me to the warmth of your chest
as if to give me all your love
You handled with care, gave me much needed
attention, and I realized that I was none of what
anyone else called me or
what I allowed myself to believe
I saw the beauty of who I am through you
Thank you for the view
Most people can't recognize treasure when they see it

———————

I've traced my purpose within
the folds of your smile
and the glint in your eye
Right now, I'm just watching you breathe
I didn't know happiness could be so filling
A daily dose of my appreciation for your
existence

The substance of your knowledge
is all that feeds me
My Soul hungered for years
until in your presence
Now I sit full
Your arms my fortress of solitude
I listen with intent
Please don't ever stop speaking
Whisper into my ears even while I sleep
Let your words penetrate and enter my mind
For what would my Dreams be without you?

Our First Place

The takeout was awful
We know better for next time
We're sitting on the floor
eating off the coffee table I put together
We're exhausted, in desperate need of a shower
and honestly, I couldn't be happier
My heart is so full, at home with you

My bare feet against the cold floor
Our intimates engaging in the wash
You're building a dresser in the bedroom
and soon it'll be time to rest
This all seems so small, so insignificant
Except everything it took to get here

September 4th

The smell of coffee lingers in the air
We're wrapped up in bed again
sweatpants and comfy socks
laughing for no reason
I think when joy spills over
that it comes out as giggles
Then all at once it's quiet
We're holding each other
soaking up the moment
We know we'll have to start the day soon
You kiss me softly and then try to move
I say five more minutes
You stay for ten

Settled In

I love how the sunset seems to linger here
It hangs on just a bit longer
Home, the concept of it has changed for me
It's become permanent
Enthralled in the routines, and the lingering smell
of garlic from last night's dinner
I love cooking for you, and the expression that
creeps on your face when you're satisfied
You know I'm watching, waiting
I love how happiness lives here
roaming fondly through every room

―――――――

We're never really here
We're always looking backward or forward
but the present gets disregarded
The smell of a book, the beauty of a flower,
the vastness that surrounds us
We're all just so used to it
that we stop giving it credit
We don't take in its splendor or comfort
We just move past it into the next scene

I love the way the early morning sun
creeps onto buildings and becomes a new skin
The way my husband smells after a shower
How soft his hair feels between my fingers
The face he makes and that little sigh of
exasperation when I stare at him too long

We tune it out like an old song
that we know the words to and love
Checked out from the present moment
as if it no longer needs our attention

Antigua

I took a shower outside today
completely vulnerable, fully exposed
Cast in a full light,
I was forced to bear witness
to the effects of my neglect, and worry
How wrong I've been
How hard on myself
With each drop, my insecurities
begrudgingly gave way
I have never felt so liberated

My lover is waiting for me
We've rediscovered something
in one another, a carnal desire
Yes, I love you, but I want you, need you
I don't think I've said that in a while
I'm sorry
I think the things we are accustomed to
we sometimes take for granted

I didn't know what it was
until I was wrapped in it
Serenity, how I've missed you
Your waves of calm
Your silent grace
Thank you for finding me here

3am in May

This city lights up for me
at least that's what I selfishly tell myself
With its radiance shining down on me,
the enormity of its structures
There's just something about it
A charm that I haven't been able
to capture in photos or in words
It's just the feeling I get when I'm in a cab
listening to the sounds of it, watching the people
or strolling through the park with Sin
There's something about living in
the veins of this city
You feel its pulse and mold
yourself to the rhythm
You belong to it, you want to belong to it
The city lights up for everyone
and we go straight for it, dreamy eyed
After being here long enough
nowhere else feels quite as lively

Fall in New York

I love moments like this
That right-after-6am beauty that
cascades itself over the still-waking city
Our living room painted in a golden-hour glow
There is just something about morning
It's a show that builds then unfolds its splendor
stealing your breath away
That's the payment, your unyielding adoration
for the work of art that is cast into the sky

Midtown

We match this place that we inhabit so fondly
with its warm tones and open space
There is no awkwardness to our silence
It's filled to the brim with adoration
We don't need to fill this peace
with empty gestures or words
I guess this is what being secure feels like
This quiet resolve, this strong assurance
of our love for one another
So, we sit holding hands, or with book and pen
Simply ourselves without reservations

First Snow

Snow is coming down by the loads
Whisking by the windowsill
You start to get dressed and
I know what's coming
Walking around till our fingers
are numb chasing that magic shot
Laughing as we slide on sidewalks
and jump over snow that's
piled up in the street
These are the moments that make me
adore you all the more
Completely out of the realm of comfort
Thrust into lungs filled with cold air
and snow-covered lashes
I love it, I love you, and that you bring me along
A partner with you on this quest
to capture this beauty
Tackling the storm and laughing right through it

Sausalito

I've desperately searched the world
for a place to cleanse my mind
It's always going, chastising, criticizing
I need a break
A moment where I focus on nothing more
than my breath and how air feels in my lungs
I've found paradise in Sausalito, but no peace
My inner critic just keeps knocking away at my
self-esteem
Things are slow paced here, but I'm moving at
full speed
Guess New York is more like an imprint than a
memory

Tucson

I was holding it all together
then you asked if I was ok
It all happened so suddenly
Just like that it was wave after wave of anguish
I just kept crying
I normally don't say much
Never wanting my gloom
to be an intrusion on anyone else's happiness
I can tell from your face that
it's washing over you
I can see it in your hesitance
to reach out and touch me
Trying to decide to come over
or let me be for a while
I sit there waiting for you to cross the
current of my emotions and be an anchor
You do, you always do,
then something quiets in me
I tell myself the storm inside
my head isn't so bad
Here in your arms I'm steady
I look at myself and see struggles
You see a fighter
I like who I am through your eyes
You're still holding me, don't stop holding me
I don't want to face it all on my own yet

October Is Ours

I remember we were in such a rush that day
You helped me with my dress
So many people make it seem like there's a
change that happens
Truth is, deciding to spend my life with you is by
far the most natural decision
that I've entered into
We stood on the sand, encased in flowers
The ocean crashed against the shore
The sun was setting
The conch shell was blown
and it brought me comfort to think
that maybe someone from whom I descended
showed up to watch our union
You're a good man; they would be
proud of my choice to have you as my partner
We held hands and took turns
staring at each other
We smiled so much, laughed so deeply
You are my happy place
this merely increased that
With a kiss it was sealed
There wasn't a more perfect way
to add a new chapter to our journey
We will always have the shore, the ocean
and October

Happy to Be Holmes

I live for these kinds of days
Rain kissing the window
Snuggled underneath your arm
I'm supposed to be paying attention
to what we're watching
but I'm taken in by your warmth
I'm basking in this blissful moment
Cups of coffee, the scent of candles
We've created our own world that
we proudly enjoy together
You catch me staring at you
An inquisitive look on your face
How can I tell you how much I love you?
How happy you make me
I just smile awkwardly then laugh
You get it
You pretend to go back to watching the show
as I simply continue to stare at you

Phuket, First Swim

The chill of the water enveloping my skin,
sliding through my fingers
The sunlight dancing on the pool's surface
With each stroke I was propelled toward
a freedom unknown to me before
Here I was, a little less afraid
My only focus being to make it to the edge,
to push myself a little harder
Coming up for air, I'm met by the sound
of waves crashing, wind rustling through
the palm trees
I look over my shoulder and catch my lover's
eyes fondly trained on me
There's no fighting the smile that's making its way
out of me from reading the pride that's
on his face
It's contagious and all-consuming, this happiness
For once I feel in control
I just want to stay here with him
In love and unison
Salt water, sun, and liberation

Summer in Paris

Sunbeams kissing my back
Dust kicking up at my heels
My sweaty palm against yours
We've found so much solace here
Happiness has burrowed and nestled inside
We've walked through halls filled with art
I must admit, I've paid more attention to your
face
The way your gaze hangs upon something you
like, the excitement, the way inspiration flows for
you so easily here
You are my favorite piece of everything
I listen to you speak and it's like no one
else is here
We are just strolling in our own world
I don't know if Paris got the best of me
or you made me fall in love with it

Bound to You

They didn't teach me what love is
There wasn't a good example set
Romance gets focused on so much,
but people forget to mention the substance
Here I am concerning myself with your health
and focusing on the minute details of your life
'cause I want you in mine
The way I'll indulge myself in the scent of your
skin and how it feels wrapped around mine
They left out the pillars that form from
the sense of stability that is created
Boring isn't ever a word that needs to be
uttered when speaking of our consistency
I don't ever think I had that before you
With you, I get to dream of kids and a home
without feeling that it's a far-fetched concept
that I've ventured into alone

I want the crow's feet from years of laughter at
jokes I've heard hundreds of times
I want the wrinkles of skin
that your fingers will still caress and adore
I want the stories we tell our offspring
and their offspring about how we met
and traveled the world
I want it all

They didn't tell me what love is
at least not one worth keeping
I've learned all the things it wasn't

and so many of the ways it shouldn't feel
They didn't tell me it could heal
They didn't tell me what love is
You're the one who showed me

Wanderlust

I came home to gray buildings and skyscrapers
only to crave something old and majestic
Europe has spoiled me
I miss the calm, I miss the quiet
The lack of pressure to rush
I gracefully glided through the days
I thought nowhere else in the world
would ever feel like home and yet
home is where I now feel out of place
A stranger among my own things
They no longer seem as important
Everything feels so different
I'm honestly just waiting for the moment
that we can go back

October in Paris

We land in the morning
Met by a darkened sky and the
quietness that envelops it
Here is where you've chosen
to celebrate our special occasion
Within days we've nestled into a routine
of spending quality time indoors or looking
out over the city
Venturing out is a thrill as we're exposed
to more and more of this city's charm
A night spent exploring, filled with photography
and a stroll along the Seine
A morning spent walking through the garden
and being captivated by the beauty of fall
Time has gotten away from us here
We lost ourselves within each other
and the adventure
Now here we are wrapped in the cool air of the
evening, gazing at the stars from our own little
slice of paradise
Laughing, kissing, and talking about the
possibilities of our future
My body an exhibition of your fingerprints
I'll leave the remainder of the night off this page
Archive the memory under beautiful and sacred

Index

Andrews McMeel Publishing
a division of Andrews McMeel Universal
1130 Walnut Street, Kansas City, Missouri 64106

www.andrewsmcmeel.com

19 20 21 22 23 BVG 10 9 8 7 6 5 4 3 2 1

ISBN: 978-1-5248-5133-0

Library of Congress Control Number: 2018966788

Editor: Patty Rice
Art Director: Holly Swayne
Production Editor: Amy Strassner
Production Manager: Cliff Koehler

ATTENTION: SCHOOLS AND BUSINESSES
Andrews McMeel books are available at quantity discounts with
bulk purchase for educational, business, or sales promotional use.
For information, please e-mail the Andrews McMeel Publishing
Special Sales Department: specialsales@amuniversal.com.